Buddhist Festivals
Through the Year

Anita Ganeri

W
FRANKLIN WATTS
LONDON • SYDNEY

© 2003 Franklin Watts

First published in Great Britain by
Franklin Watts
96 Leonard Street
LONDON EC2A 4XD

Franklin Watts Australia
45–51 Huntley Street
Alexandria
NSW 2015

ISBN: 0 7496 4801 5
A CIP catalogue record for this book is available from the British Library

Printed in Hong Kong, China

Editor: Kate Banham   Designer: Joelle Wheelwright
Art Direction: Jonathan Hair   Illustrations: Peter Bull
Picture Research: Diana Morris   Faith Consultant: Clive Erricker
Educational Consultant: Alan Brown

Acknowledgements
The publishers would like to thank the following for permission to
reproduce photographs in this book:
David Cummings/Eye Ubiquitous: 6, 21b; John Dakers/Eye Ubiquitous: 14;
Nick Dawson/World Religions Photo Library: 24, 25t; Bennett Dean/Eye Ubiquitous: 7b;
A. Deutsch/Trip: 11; Gapper/World Religions Photo Library: 8, 22; C. McCooey/Trip:
26; Christine Osborne/World Religions Photo Library: 10, 13, 16b, 18b, 19, 20t, 20b;
Tim Page/Eye Ubiquitous: front cover, 12, 16t, 18t; H. Rogers/Trip: 17; Paul Seheult/Eye
Ubiquitous: 7t; Pam Smith/Eye Ubiquitous: 23; Superbild/A1pix: 15; A. Tovey/Trip: 27b;
Julia Waterlow/Eye Ubiquitous: 9, 25b.

Whilst every attempt has been made to clear copyright, should there be any inadvertent
omission please apply in the first instance to the publisher regarding rectification.

Contents

Words printed in **bold** are explained in the glossary.

Introduction

Buddhists are people who follow the teachings of a man called Siddhattha Gotama who lived in India about 2,500 years ago. He became the Buddha, which means 'enlightened one'. Today, there are about 400 million Buddhists. Very few still live in India where Buddhism began. But in some other Asian countries, such as Sri Lanka and Thailand, Buddhism is the main religion. Buddhism has also become popular in North America and Europe.

This Buddhist monk is studying 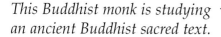 *an ancient Buddhist sacred text.*

Five promises

In their daily lives, Buddhists make five important precepts, or promises:

1. Not to harm living things.
2. Not to take what is not freely given.
3. Not to misuse the senses.
4. Not to speak wrongly.
5. Not to use drugs or drink alcohol.

Life of the Buddha

Siddhattha Gotama was born in about 480BCE. The son of a king, he grew up in great luxury. But one day, on a chariot ride, he saw an old man, a sick man and a dead man. Siddhattha was shocked at such suffering. Then he saw a wandering **monk**, who seemed happy despite having nothing. Siddhattha decided to follow the monk's example and find the answer to life's suffering. That night, he left the palace and began his search for the truth. After many years, he gained **enlightenment**. He saw why people suffered and how they could be helped. For the rest of his life, he travelled around India, living as a wandering monk, teaching people what he had learned.

Buddhist practice

Buddhists practise their religion at home or in the **vihara** (temple or **monastery**). To show their respect, they kneel or bow in front of an image of the Buddha. They make offerings of flowers, incense and candles, and **chant** verses from the sacred texts. This is called *puja*. Buddhists do not worship the Buddha as a god but honour him as a very special human being.

········▶

A woman and girl offering incense to the Buddha at a street shrine in Thailand.

Buddhist beliefs

The first part of the Buddha's teaching is called the Four Noble Truths. These say that life is full of **dukkha**, or suffering, because people are never content with what they have. The way to end suffering is to follow the Noble Eightfold Path. The steps on the path are:

1. Right understanding – of the Buddha's teachings.
2. Right thought – thinking kind thoughts.
3. Right speech – not speaking angrily or telling lies.
4. Right action – not stealing or harming others.
5. Right livelihood – doing a job that does not harm others.
6. Right effort – working to do the right thing.
7. Right awareness – being alert and aware.
8. Right concentration – training your mind to be calm.

The eight-spoked wheel represents the Noble Eightfold Path.

Buddhist Festivals

There are many festivals throughout the Buddhist year. Many mark important times in the Buddha's life or events from Buddhist history. Some are celebrated by Buddhists everywhere. Others are special to particular groups of Buddhists (see opposite). Because Buddhism has spread to many countries, festivals vary from place to place and are greatly influenced by local customs and traditions. At festival times, Buddhists visit their local vihara to take gifts for the monks and **nuns**. They take part in *puja* and listen to talks about the Buddha's teaching.

These Buddhists are giving gifts to the monks in their local temple in London, England.

The Buddhist calendar

There is no set Buddhist calendar. Early Buddhists adopted an ancient Indian calendar. Later, as Buddhism moved out of India, festivals were arranged according to the calendar of the different countries. Most Buddhist festivals, except for those celebrated in Japan, are based on the lunar year. The lunar calendar is shorter than the everyday, Western calendar so an extra month is added every few years to bring the two into line. (See page 28 for one set of names for the months of the Buddhist year).

Buddhist groups

All Buddhists share the same basic beliefs but they have different ways of interpreting the Buddha's teachings. The two main Buddhist schools are **Theravada** and **Mahayana** but there are many other groups.

• Theravada means 'the way of the elders'. Theravada Buddhists stick strictly to the teachings of Siddhattha Gotama, the historical Buddha. Theravada Buddhism is mainly practised in Sri Lanka, Myanmar, Thailand, Cambodia and Laos.

• Mahayana means 'great vehicle'. Mahayana Buddhists believe in many different Buddhas and in god-like figures, called *bodhisattvas*. Mahayana Buddhism is mainly practised in Nepal, China, Japan, Korea and Vietnam.

• Tibetan Buddhism is a type of Mahayana Buddhism mixed with many colourful rites and rituals. Buddhism came to Tibet from India in the 7th century CE. The Dalai Lama, who now lives in exile in India, is the leader of Tibet's Buddhists.

• The Friends of the Western Buddhist Order (FWBO) was started in Britain in 1967 by an Englishman, Dennis Lingwood, who became a Buddhist monk and took the name Sangharakshita. He developed a kind of Buddhism better suited to the modern, Western world.

Full Moon Days

Many Buddhist festivals happen at the time of the full moon, when the most important events in the Buddha's life are said to have occurred. This was also when the monks met to recite the rules of the monastic order by which they lived. In the West, Buddhists often celebrate on the nearest Sunday so they do not have to take time off from work or school to visit the vihara. They often wear simple, white clothes as a sign of purity.

·····················▶

Many Buddhist celebrations involve acting out traditional stories.

Wesak

The festival of *Wesak* falls in April or May. This is the most important time of the year for Theravada Buddhists everywhere, when they remember the Buddha's birthday, his enlightenment and passing into **nirvana**. Tradition says that these three events all took place on the full moon of the month of *Vesaka* in the Indian calendar, from which *Wesak* gets its name (see page 28). It is also called Buddha Day. Mahayana Buddhists celebrate these three events on separate days. At *Wesak*, Buddhists try to remember the Buddha by living up to his teachings, especially by being kind, generous and **compassionate**.

This painting from Korea shows Siddhattha sitting under the Bodhi *tree, where he gained enlightenment and became the Buddha.*

Seeing the truth

After leaving the palace (see page 6), Siddhattha began his search for the truth. For six years, he lived in the forest with five holy men. Their life was very hard. Siddhattha's clothes were so rough they made his skin sore and he ate so little he looked like a skeleton. But still he did not find the truth. One day, he left the forest and made his way to the village of Bodh Gaya. There he sat down under a tall tree (the *Bodhi* tree) and began to meditate. During the night, Mara, the evil one, tried to tempt him away from his search. But nothing Mara could do could hurt Siddhattha. The poisoned arrows and burning spears which Mara hurled at him fell like petals around his feet. Finally, Mara fled. Then, at last, Siddhattha gained enlightenment and saw the truth about how things really were. It was like a light going on in the darkness. Now he knew why people suffered and how they could be helped. Siddhattha had become the Buddha, the enlightened one.

The Buddha passes away

When he was about 80 years old, the Buddha was ready to die. Just before he died, he called his monks together and told them not to be sad. He reminded them of the teaching that everything changes and passes away. He told them to go and carry on his teaching. It would now be their guide.

This huge statue in Sri Lanka shows the Buddha's parinirvana, *or passing away.*

Celebrating Wesak

In Buddhist countries, *Wesak* is celebrated on the day of the full moon in April or May, and may be a public holiday. In other countries, it is celebrated on the nearest weekend. Many Buddhists make offerings at the vihara and take gifts for the monks. Generosity is very important for Buddhists. They hope that it will help them reach enlightenment. In the vihara there is a special *Wesak puja*, and the monks give talks about the Buddha's life. Some people send cards or exchange small gifts.

In Sri Lanka, small oil lamps are lit to celebrate Wesak.

Honouring the Buddha

When Buddhists visit the vihara, they take offerings of lights, flowers and incense to place before the image of the Buddha in the shrine room. Each of these offerings has a special meaning:
• Lights: these may be oil lamps, lanterns or candles. They stand for the Buddha's enlightenment.
• Flowers: these look beautiful but they soon fade and die. This reminds Buddhists that nothing lasts for ever.
• Incense: the sweet smell of the incense is a reminder of the sweetness of the Buddha's teaching.

Wesak lights

Wesak is celebrated differently from country to country. In Sri Lanka, people decorate their homes and viharas with lanterns or candles. Huge, illuminated displays light up the streets. These lights are symbols of the Buddha's enlightenment. They light up the darkness, just as the Buddha's teaching lights up the world. In Thailand, *Wesak* ends with a candlelit procession. People walk around the vihara three times, to stand for the Buddha, the **dhamma** (his teaching) and the **sangha** (the Buddhist community). These three things are called the Three Jewels of Buddhism because they are so precious.

It is traditional to hang up colourful lanterns to mark the Buddha's birthday.

Jataka stories

Buddhists believe that people live many lives. This is called **reincarnation**. At *Wesak*, Buddhist children listen to stories about the Buddha's past lives. These are called *Jataka* stories. They help children to understand the Buddha's teachings. The Buddha often appears as an animal to teach a particular lesson. In one story, the Buddha was born as a lion. One day, a jackal saved his life. In return, the lion protected the jackal and helped him to hunt for food. This teaches children the value of friendship, and the importance of doing good turns.

Wesak cards

Many Buddhists exchange greetings cards at *Wesak*. Try making some of your own. Decorate them with pictures of the Buddha, or with a **lotus** blossom or eight-spoked **dhamma** **wheel**. Write 'Happy *Wesak*' inside.

O-bon

O*-bon* is a Mahayana Buddhist festival which is celebrated in Japan in July or August. This is a time for remembering people who have died and welcoming their spirits home for their yearly visit. But it is not a time for being sad. Buddhists believe that when you die, you are born again in another body. Ancestors are thought of in a happy way and *O-bon* is a very joyous festival.

These women and children are performing a traditional folk dance for O-bon.

The story of *O-bon*

There was once a very holy monk, called Maudgalyayana, who was one of the Buddha's chief followers. When his mother died, her spirit was banished to hell because of a lie she had told. Maudgalyayana visited her there and found her in a pitiful state. The only person who could save her was the Buddha himself. Maudgalyayana gave a feast as an offering to the Buddha and all the monks. Then the Buddha pulled Maudgalyayana's mother out of hell with a rope.

O-bon celebrations

Traditionally at *O-bon* people return to their family village for the three days of the festival. On the first day, they decorate their houses with lanterns, place herbs and flowers on the family shrine, and light small bonfires to welcome the spirits home. On the second day, there is a sumptuous feast. Everyone in the village gathers in a circle to take part in a traditional folk dance. There are also games to play, including a tug-of-war, to remind people of the story of Maudgalyayana and his mother. On the third day, people make offerings of fruit and flowers at their family shrine, and ask for the Buddha's blessing on their ancestors. Then it is time to say goodbye and the spirits depart again. *O-bon* is a very busy time for Buddhist monks. They try to visit as many homes as possible to chant verses from the Buddhist sacred texts.

Floating spirit lights

At the end of the *O-bon* festival, miniature boats made from paper or straw and filled with tiny candles are set sailing on lakes and rivers to carry the spirits back to their world. Make your own floating spirit lights. Fill a glass bowl with water. Float small, flat candles on the surface for a glittering effect. Warning: do not leave burning candles unattended.

People pray before casting the spirit lights adrift.

Poson

The festival of *Poson* takes place on the day of the full moon in June or July. It is celebrated by Theravada Buddhists from Sri Lanka. The festival marks the arrival of Buddhism in Sri Lanka.

The story of *Poson*

Buddhism was brought to Sri Lanka in the 3rd century BCE. The Sri Lankan king asked Ashoka, the Buddhist emperor of India, to send a monk to the island to teach him about Buddhism. Ashoka sent his own son, Mahinda. After listening to Mahinda, the king converted to Buddhism. In Sri Lanka, *Poson* is celebrated with a colourful procession. Huge floats carry images telling the story of Mahinda and the king. In the West, Sri Lankan Buddhists celebrate with a day-long programme of chanting, **meditation** and talks about Mahinda in the vihara.

Tree of knowledge

The tree beneath which the Buddha gained enlightenment is called the *Bodhi* tree. The word '*bodhi*' means knowledge or wisdom. A cutting of the original *Bodhi* tree at Bodh Gaya was taken to Sri Lanka by Ashoka's daughter, Sanghamitta, who was a Buddhist nun. She planted it in the city of Anuradhapura where it is still growing today. The city is a very holy place for Buddhist **pilgrims** to visit.

The sacred Bodhi *tree in Anuradhapura.*

Asala

In July or August, Theravada Buddhists celebrate the festival of *Asala*. This festival remembers the first talk, or sermon, that the Buddha gave after his enlightenment.

The Deer Park in Sarnath, India, where the Buddha preached his first sermon.

The Wheel of Law

After his enlightenment, the Buddha made his way to the Deer Park near the holy city of Varanasi. There he met the five holy men who had been his companions in the forest (see page 10). That evening, he gave his first talk, called the Turning of the Wheel of Law. He taught that when you die, you are reborn in a different body. What your next life is like depends on your actions, good and bad, in this world. Everyone is caught up in an endless cycle of life, death and rebirth. To break free and find peace, people need to understand the Four Noble Truths and to follow the Noble Eightfold Path, a middle way between extreme luxury and extreme hardship (see page 7). After the teaching, the five holy men became the Buddha's first followers.

The festival of the tooth

In Kandy, Sri Lanka, there are spectacular processions through the streets to celebrate *Asala*. They last for 10–15 days. At the height of the celebrations, more than one hundred beautifully decorated elephants parade through the city streets, accompanied by dancers, drummers and acrobats. The grandest elephant carries a copy of a golden casket on its back. It contains a very precious **relic** – a tooth which is said to have belonged to the Buddha himself. The original casket is kept safely in the nearby Temple of the Tooth, where it is honoured daily. Tradition says that the ruler of Sri Lanka has to have the tooth under his protection in order to be the true king.

The elephants taking part in the procession wear beautiful coverings.

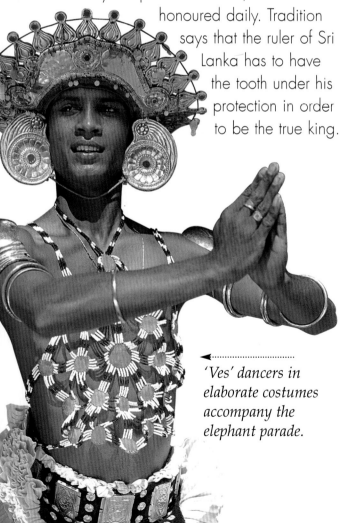

'Ves' dancers in elaborate costumes accompany the elephant parade.

The Buddha's First Sermon

At Asala, the whole of the Buddha's sermon is chanted to mark the beginning of the Buddha's teaching. This is part of it:

'Monks, these two extremes should not be practised by those who have to leave their homes behind. What are the two? There is devotion to great luxury... And there is devotion to great hardship. Avoiding these extremes, you should follow the Middle Path. It gives vision and knowledge, and leads to calmness, to insight, to enlightenment and to *nirvana*.'

Kathina

athina is a Theravada Buddhist festival which takes place in October or November. It is a time when **lay Buddhists** visit their local vihara to give gifts of new robes to the monks at a special ceremony.

The Buddha and his disciples dressed in traditional robes.

How *Kathina* began

Kathina takes place at the end of the rainy season in Asian countries, such as Sri Lanka. During this time, the rains made it difficult for the Buddha and his monks to travel and teach. They stayed in a vihara until the weather improved. This was known as the Rains Retreat. According to the Buddhist sacred texts, a group of monks was travelling to spend the Rains Retreat with the Buddha. But the rains started early and they could not reach him. To cheer them up, the Buddha told them to collect some cloth for robes and to sew a new robe for one of the monks. He knew that this act of sharing and generosity would lift their spirits.

A new robe

The main gift given at *Kathina* is a new robe. On the day of the festival, people arrive early at the vihara for the robe-giving ceremony. After *puja*, cloth for the robe is offered to the monks. They decide among themselves who deserves it most and then make it into a robe. People give the robe to thank the monks for inspiring them by their own example to live a good, holy life. People also hope that, in doing a good deed, they will earn merit for themselves which will help them on their path to enlightenment. The new robe also marks a fresh start for the monks after the Rains Retreat. In Thailand, *Kathina* celebrations last for a week. During this time, the king and royal family visit nine different viharas. In each, a *Kathina* robe is offered to the most virtuous monk.

▲ *Buddhist monks helping each other to put on their robes.*

At Kathina, *Buddhists give offerings of money, pinned to a money tree.*

Receiving the Robe

A verse spoken by the monks as they receive the Kathina *robe:*

'Those who are wise, generous
And free from selfishness
Are generous at the right times.
Then what is given to those
Who are virtuous [the monks]
Is an offering of great purity and worth.
Those who show compassion
Or perform generous acts
Also make a great offering
And they also share in this merit.
And those good deeds
Bring about good fortune in the life
to come.'

Monks and nuns

The Buddha himself lived as a monk and some Buddhists choose to follow in his footsteps. They leave their homes and possessions behind, and become monks or nuns. They lead strict, simple lives, according to a set of more than 200 rules. They spend their time studying the sacred texts, meditating, running the vihara and helping the local community to lead better lives. In Theravada countries, they rely on gifts from local people for their food. In addition to the Five Precepts (see page 6), monks make five extra promises. These are:

1. Not eating after midday.
2. Not singing or dancing.
3. Not using perfume or cosmetics.
4. Not sleeping in a soft bed.
5. Not handling money.

Young monks like these have to go through a special ceremony before entering the monastery.

A monk's possessions

Traditionally, monks are only allowed to own eight items. These are called the Eight Requisites, or needs, and were set down long ago by the Buddha. They are:
1. Robes (saffron – for Theravada monks, or maroon – for Mahayana monks).
2. A belt.
3. A needle and thread.
4. An alms bowl.
5. A walking stick.
6. A razor.
7. A toothpick.
8. A water filter.

An alms bowl

Robes

A razor

Sangha Day

*S*angha Day is one of the main festivals marked by the Friends of the Western Buddhist Order, or FWBO (see page 9). It falls on the day of the full moon in November and celebrates the love and friendship shared by the *sangha*, or Buddhist community. The *sangha* is one of the Three Jewels of Buddhism (see page 13).

Celebrating *Sangha* Day

On *Sangha* Day, the *mitras* (friends) visit their local Buddhist centre for a day of celebration. After lunch, people sit together and talk about their hopes and fears. They believe that it is important to share their feelings with each other. In the evening, there is a special *puja* in the shrine room. It is beautifully decorated with red banners and flowers for the occasion. People sit in front of the image of the Buddha and chant or meditate. Then they renew their vows (see below). Often people exchange small gifts, and there may be a firework display.

A Western Buddhist lighting a candle at a temple in London, England.

Buddhist vows

When someone becomes a Buddhist, they make a commitment to the Three Jewels by reciting the following vows. They also repeat these vows as part of daily practice.

' I go to the Buddha as my refuge.
I go to the *Dhamma* as my refuge.
I go to the *Sangha* as my refuge.'

A refuge is a place where a person can feel safe and happy. It is also someone you can trust, like the Buddha or the Buddhist community.

Losar

In February, Tibetan Buddhists celebrate the New Year, with the festival of *Losar*. Before the Chinese invasion of Tibet in the 1950s, *Losar* celebrations lasted for 15 days, and huge crowds gathered in the monasteries. Today, Tibetan refugees in India usually celebrate for three days.

Prayer flags fluttering from a Tibetan Buddhist temple in Nepal.

Prayers and offerings

At *Losar*, people visit their local temple or monastery to honour the Buddha and make offerings of *khatas* (white greeting scarves) and food to the monks. In the shrine room, they bow or kneel before the image of the Buddha, and light yak-butter lamps. The monks chant from the sacred texts and burn bundles of sweet-smelling juniper and cedar branches. In Tibet, brightly-coloured prayer flags flutter from the rooftops of many homes and monasteries. Written on them are hundreds of prayers. As the wind blows, it carries the prayers into the world. At *Losar*, old prayer flags are taken down and replaced with new ones.

New Year celebrations

Losar is a happy time for visiting friends and family, and remembering the Buddha's life. It is also a time for leaving bad luck behind, and starting a fresh, new year. *Losar* celebrations begin a few days before New Year's Day. Houses and monasteries are spring-cleaned and decorated. New clothes are made and old quarrels settled. On New Year's Day, people get up early and visit the river or well because water collected on that day is thought to have special powers.

*A **Cham** dancer dressed in a spectacular costume.*

Sacred dancing

Traditionally, in Tibet, festivals were marked by spectacular performances of the sacred *Cham* dance. These dances were held in the courtyards of the great monasteries, and symbolised the victory of good over evil. Certain characters from Tibetan mythology always appeared, dressed in elaborate costumes and masks. Among them were Yama, the god of death, the Black Hat priest and the skeleton lords. The dances were intended to drive out the evil spirits of the old year, and ensure a good start to the new one.

Butter sculptures

Tormas are offerings made from barley flour dough, covered with sculptures made from yak butter. Huge *tormas* are prepared by Tibetan monks for festivals such as *Losar*. The decorations include lucky symbols, heavenly beings and scenes from the Buddha's life. Try making your own butter sculpture in the shape of a flower, the sun or the moon. Instead of butter, you can use modelling clay or plasticine in different colours. Leave your sculpture to dry hard, then decorate it with paint or glitter.

▲ *This monk is making a butter sculpture for the New Year* Losar *celebrations.*

Secret dumplings

At *Losar*, people eat special foods such as *gutuk*, or dumpling soup. The dumplings are stuffed with hidden ingredients to show what the New Year will bring. For example, if you find coal inside your dumpling, it means a bad year ahead. If you find salt, however, it means that you will have good luck.

These Tibetan Buddhists are making cakes from tsampa *flour for* Losar.

Flour-throwing

Tsampa (barley flour) is a staple part of the Tibetan diet, and is often eaten mixed with yak butter. Throwing *tsampa* into the air is an important *Losar* custom. Guests are presented with a pot of *tsampa* when they visit a person's home. They take a pinch and throw it into the air to honour the Buddha and bring good luck. People also visit the viharas and throw handfuls of *tsampa* into the air to welcome in the New Year.

Hana-Matsuri

Hana-Matsuri is a very important festival for Mahayana Buddhists in Japan. It falls in April and celebrates the birthday of the Buddha.

The Buddha's birthday

According to the story, Queen Maya, the Buddha's mother, had a dream in which she saw a white elephant with six tusks come down from the sky. It was a sign that she was to have a son who would grow up to be great and good. When the time came for the baby to be born, the Queen travelled to her parents' house. On the way, she stopped in a beautiful garden called Lumbini Grove, which was filled with flowers and birdsong. There, the Buddha was born.

Flower festival

Hana-Matsuri is also a flower festival which marks the coming of spring and the blooming of the cherry trees. The word '*hana*' is Japanese for flower and '*matsuri*' means festival.

This lantern has been decorated with cherry blossom pictures for Hana-Matsuri.

The cherry blossom is the national flower of Japan and people flock to parks and gardens to see the best displays. The blossoms look beautiful but are delicate. After just a few days they wilt and die. This reminds people of the Buddha's teaching that everything changes. At *Hana-Matsuri*, children wear flowers in their hair and the streets are decorated with streamers made to look like cherry blossom.

Cherry blossom

To make some branches of cherry blossom, you will need some twigs or branches and some small circles of white or pink tissue paper. Fold each circle in half, then in quarters and twist the bottom to make a flower shape. Stick your paper blossoms on to the branches.

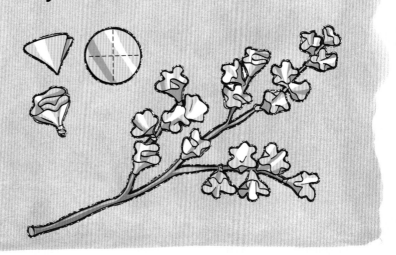

Celebrating *Hana-Matsuri*

At *Hana-Matsuri,* models of flower gardens are set up in the temple courtyards. They remind people of the garden in which the Buddha is said to have been born. An image of the baby Buddha is placed in the model garden, and visitors to the vihara pour spoonfuls of specially scented tea made from hydrangea leaves over the image. This is a reminder of the perfumed water which the gods sent down from heaven to bathe the baby Buddha. A large, white, papier-mâché elephant is also placed there to remind people of Queen Maya's dream. *Hana-Matsuri* is a happy occasion. In the vihara grounds, there are story-tellers, acrobats and folk-dancers, and stalls selling fish soup, rice-balls, paper umbrellas and lucky charms.

Costumed story-tellers for **Hana-Matsuri.**

27

Festival Calendar

Month	Festival
April/May	*Wesak* (Theravada)
July/August	*O-bon* (Mahayana/Japan)
June/July	*Poson* (Theravada)
July/August	*Asala* (Theravada)
October/November	*Kathina* (Theravada)
November	*Sangha* Day (FWBO)
February	*Losar* (Mahayana/Tibet)
April	*Hana-Matsuri* (Mahayana/Japan)

Buddhist months

In Pali, an ancient Indian language similar to that thought to have been spoken by the Buddha, the months of the Buddhist lunar year are:

Citta	(March/April)
Vesaka	(April/May)
Jettha	(May/June)
Asalha	(June/July)
Savana	(July/August)
Potthabada	(August/September)
Assayuja	(September/October)
Kattika	(October/November)
Maggasira	(November/December)
Pussa	(December/January)
Maga	(January/February)
Phagguna	(February/March)

Glossary

Chanting Half-speaking, half-singing the words of a sacred text. Chanting is very calming and peaceful to do and to listen to.

Compassionate Kind and caring.

Dhamma The teachings of the Buddha.

Dhamma wheel An eight-spoked wheel. Each of the eight spokes stands for a step on the Noble Eightfold Path.

Dukkha Suffering or being unhappy with life.

Enlightenment Realising the true meaning of life, like waking up from a deep sleep.

Jataka One of a popular collection of stories about the Buddha's past lives.

Lay Buddhist A Buddhist who is not a monk or nun.

Lotus A water-lily. For Buddhists, it is a symbol of enlightenment.

Mahayana One of the main schools of Buddhism, practised in Nepal, China, Japan, Korea and Vietnam.

Meditate To clear your mind so that you feel calm and relaxed.

Monasteries Places where monks live, work and study.

Monk A man who gives up his home and possessions to follow a religious way of life.

Nirvana A state of perfect peace and stillness reached by those who have become enlightened.

Nun A woman who gives up her home and possessions to follow a religious way of life.

Pilgrims People who make a special journey to a sacred place, such as a temple or monastery.

Puja The way in which Buddhists honour the Buddha by making offerings of flowers, lights and incense.

Reincarnation To be born again in a different body.

Relic Something which once belonged to a holy person.

Sangha The Buddhist community which includes monks, nuns and lay Buddhists.

Sutta A short sacred text. The word 'sutta' means thread.

Theravada One of the main schools of Buddhism, practised in Sri Lanka, Myanmar, Thailand, Cambodia and Laos.

Vihara A Buddhist temple or monastery.

Further Resources

Books

Celebrations! Wesak
Anita Ganeri, Heinemann, 2001

Storyteller: Buddhist Stories
Anita Ganeri, Evans Brothers, 2001

Celebration!
Barnabas and Annabel Kindersley,
Dorling Kindersley, 1997

Festivals in World Religions
The Shap Working Party on World
Religions in Education, 1998

Introducing Religions: Buddhism
Sue Penney, Heinemann, 1997

Beliefs and Cultures: Buddhism
Anita Ganeri, Watts, 1996

Websites

www.festivals.com
Information about festivals,
holy days and holidays.

www.buddhanet.net
All aspects of Buddhism and
Buddhist festivals.

www.fwbo.org/festivals
Festivals of the Friends of the
Western Buddhist Order.

www.abm.ndirect.co.uk
Theravada festivals in Thailand.

Index